Scotland

HOME *of* GOLF

Photography by **Iain M. Lowe**

and **Christopher J. Lowe**

Text and Illustrations by **David Joy**

The Old Course 3rd tee to green.

 it be a crisp winter's morning, with a frost barely in retreat, or a glorious, golden late evening in summer, with the sun on the horizon and midnight in sight, Scotland and golf share the most unique and enduring of relationships. One that, at nearly 600 years, has existed longer than many nations, and yet with the coming of each day, a new feeling of discovery.

In this book, father/son duo of Iain & Chris Lowe are teaming up again with historian/illustrator David Joy to bring to life the ever-evolving story of golf in Scotland. From its earliest days to present times, encompassing the rich history and experiences lived along the way. Played on "links" land that has itself journeyed from being "of no other use", to the most desirable of locations. All conveyed using varying tools from the age-old pencil to the latest in drone technology.

Through his unrivalled historical knowledge, Joy captures the spirit and history of the game, supported by his warm and detailed illustrations. Chronicling the good and the great who have, over hundreds of years, sought to improve the courses, equipment and ability for all of us to enjoy this game.

As fully licenced drone pilots through the CAA, the Lowes take their cameras where no helicopter can, capturing not just the innate beauty of links courses, but also conveying the architecture and challenges that are unique to this form of golf. For links golf can be an exacting test, it's true, with success and failure distributed in uneven and sometimes arbitrary fashion. But also it is here where the soul of golf resides.

With four new Championship courses opening over the last two decades, and another well-known name ascending new heights following a major redesign, the story of golf in Scotland continues to be written.

For it is not that Scotland was the Home of Golf, it still is.

All Enquiries should be addressed to:
Iain Lowe Photography
St Andrews Studio
4 Bassaguard Business Park
St Andrews
Fife KY16 8AL
UK

ISBN 978-1-5272-6956-9

By email—chris@scottishgolflibrary.com
By phone—011 44 (0) 1 334 477703
Web site—www.scottishgolflibrary.com

© All photography and book concept—Iain & Chris Lowe
© All illustrations and historical text—David Joy
Illustrations from *Joy of Golf* book

Designed by Savitski Design, Ann Arbor, Michigan USA
www.savitskidesign.com

Printed by Donning Company, Brookfield, Missouri USA
www.donning.com

Contents

Although we need a low sun to highlight the nuances of links golf, it is possible that, this being Scotland, you may experience some inclement weather! Of course, this is the extreme and it is unlikely that you will suffer such dire conditions.

Introduction

This book is unashamedly designed to brighten your day; to re-kindle happy memories of previous trips or maintain your desire to visit Scotland with club and ball. We strive to showcase the selected fourteen links courses, from the air and ground, in a way that is interesting and captivating. The low sun aiding the understanding of the golfing challenge and the beauty of the location. Yes, just fourteen links golf courses but each a treasure to be revealed; names old and familiar or new and exciting—all have impacted the evolution of the game and are deserving of their place in this book.

Then there is the history. For this we look back over some six hundred years with brief observations of the key occurrences and greatest influencers and players to have walked these links. All of this is supported by hand-drawn illustrations, an artform that we believe is far better than photography when reflecting on the goliaths of our game.

To win a Major championship is a considerable achievement, or tournament success on the tour— either side of the Atlantic. But there have always been players who stand tall in this company, whose record of wins separates them from others. These players have dominated their time, frequently in competition with others of equal status. To these players we will devote more attention, bigger illustrations and more extensive commentary to explain their status.

Old Tom Morris

Finally there is a continual underlying theme of golf courses getting longer.

This illustration is the first I did relating to golf in 1970. It was taken from a photograph by Thomas Rodger on the "Home Hole" green on the Old Course. It shows the winner Mr. Robert Chambers and the beaten finalist David Wallace. They are surrounded by local folk, including Sir Hugh Lyon Playfair in top hat with Allan Robertson and Tom Morris who helped organise the event, hovering in behind him.

I decided recently to add Molinari's winning putt at Carnoustie and to draw a friendly wave from Bobby Locke and Seve Ballesteros. I witnessed their wins at St Andrews in 1955 and 1984. I added Ben Hogan walking out of the scene with an intense look of concentration in winning the Carnoustie Open in 1953. I included Watson and Nicklaus walking off from their "Epic Dual Under the Sun" at Turnberry in 1977, when

Tom Watson emerged after a classic battle for his second of four out of five wins of the Championship on the Links of Scotland—Carnoustie '75, Turnberry '77, Muirfield '80, and Troon '82, which I am proud will all feature in this book among many classic links which the Lowes have distinctly captured. — DAVID JOY

The exceptional golfers keep on pushing the boundaries, quite literally. Their length off the tee taking bunkers out of play—result, courses get longer, new bunkers added. The ease of escape from bunkers—result, bunkers get deeper. Some courses included in this book only came to the Open rota because of changes they made to make them relevant in that era, and they now have to keep making changes. The roundabout keeps on turning.

The ground around these historic links courses is often limited, thus only so much length can be added. It is a dilemma that challenges even those who embrace technology.

This struggle between tradition and technology has continued for nearly 200 hundred year and, given the increased driving distances of today, will be unlikely to diminish.

— IAIN LOWE

A Timeline of Golf

There are references to the playing of golf (or gowf, gouffe, kolf, goff) on the Links from the 15th century in St Andrews.

1457 – King James II's Scottish Parliament banned golf and football as they interfered with archery practice, an important weapon of war against the English.

1470 – King James III's Parliament affirmed this act.

1491 – King James IV's Parliament once again sought to bring this into force.

1502 – The Act was repealed following peace with England, the King purchased clubs from a bowmaker in Perth.

Early 16th Century golf recorded by Aberdeen and Carnoustie.

Early 17th Century golf recorded by the linksland of Dornoch.

The "linksland" is named after the dormant ground that links the sea with the arable land.

1744 – the formation of the Honourable Company of Edinburgh Golfers.

1754 – the founding of the St Andrews Society of Golfers (changed its name to the Royal and Ancient in 1834).

1764 – the official nine holes of St Andrews are set.

1780 – The Society of Golfers in Aberdeen.

1815 – Kingsbarns Golfing Society.

1832 – The North Berwick Golf Club.

1840s – trains linking up the linksland.

1847 – ten holes laid out at Carnoustie.

1848 – feathery golf ball replaced by gutta.

1851 – twelve holes laid out at Prestwick.

1860 – first Open Championship at Prestwick.

1867 – Carnoustie converts to eighteen holes and Young Tom wins its first professional tournament, aged sixteen.

1870 – St Andrews converts to eighteen holes.

1873 – first Open at St Andrews.

1875 – Tom Morris Jr. having won four Opens dies aged 24.

1884 – Prestwick converts to eighteen holes.

1886 – Dornoch is laid out.

1888 – As is Troon.

1890 – Goose necks and rutting iron are replaced by brassys, bulgers and niblicks!

1891 – Muirfield was laid out. Club moved from Musselburgh.

1892 – first Open at Muirfield.

1893 – Cruden Bay is laid out.

1894 to 1914 – the emergence of "The Triumvirate" — Taylor, Vardon, and Braid.

1902 – New ball the "Haskell" added to considerable length in the drive.

1920 to 1934 – the "American Invasion".

1923 – first Open at Troon.

1925 – last Open at Prestwick.

1940 to 1945 – no Opens played because of the Second World War.

1946 – Sam Snead U.S.A. wins St Andrews Open.

1960 – 100th Open Anniversary at St Andrews.

1960s – the emergence of the "Big Three" — Player, Palmer, and Nicklaus. Winners of the Open in Scotland, Player 1959 Muirfield, Palmer 1961 Troon, Nicklaus 1966 Muirfield and 1970 and 1978 St Andrews.

1995 – Tiger Woods arrived to play the Scottish Open at Carnoustie and the Open at St Andrews.

2000 and 2005 – Tiger Woods wins at St Andrews.

2000 – Kingsbarns as a new course was laid out using part of the original site.

Another three major constructions recently

2009 – Castle Stuart.

2012 – Trump International.

2020 – Dumbarnie.

An aerial view of the 1st green-to-tee and 16th tee-to-green.

Carnoustie

So, of all the major Scottish courses featuring in this book, why start with Carnoustie?

Well, it heralded a dramatic change and advance for golf in the late 1840s when the linkslands were "linked" up by trains and the new gutta ball replaced the feathery—suddenly the course was accessible and the ball was affordable. In 1847 a group of golfers (mainly from around Perth, St Andrews, and Montrose) invited Allan Robertson and Tom Morris to lay out an official ten-hole course on behalf of the Caledonian Club at Carnoustie—ten miles above Dundee on the east coast on the way up to Aberdeen.

Carnoustie acquired more ground in 1866, and asked Morris to adjust the ten-hole course and bring it up to eighteen. It was a family affair for the Morrises as George Morris (brother of Tom) was in charge of the newly laid out course.

Carnoustie did not advertise itself during the Victorian era, as it was busy enough with the four clubs that had grown up beside it.

The Royal and Ancient (R&A) took over the sole responsibility of running the Open in 1920. Ten years later they invited James Braid to bring the course up to championship standard by repositioning the greens and tees, and adding a few well-placed bunkers, ready for Carnoustie's first Open in 1931. Tommy Armor the "Silver Scot" emerged victorious,

In 1867 Carnoustie held its first professional tournament, Young Tom Morris emerging victorious at just 16 years of age.

Ben Hogan's victory at Carnoustie in the 1953 Open was the only professional visit he would ever make to these shores; it came after a mere two weeks of practice to gain experience of the vastly different conditions of links golf. Regardless, Hogan would put in a performance for the ages. On a course which to this day is still considered the toughest on the Open rota, Hogan improved his score on every round, culminating with one of the great final rounds in Open Championship history, a course record 68 to lift the Claret Jug at the first attempt. In doing so Hogan also became only the second man in history to achieve the career grand slam.

he had emigrated from Edinburgh nine years ago and taken American citizenship. Englishman Henry Cotton won in 1937.

The next time the Open was played in Carnoustie, American Ben Hogan made his sole appearance when winning in 1953. Fifteen years went by before South African Gary Player won his second Open title in 1968. Tom Watson won his first of five Championships starting off in Carnoustie in 1975 after a play-off. He won three more in Scotland: Turnberry '77, Muirfield '80 and Troon '82.

Carnoustie is considered the most difficult finish in all the Open courses and created drama in many a memorable Championship hosted there in recent years.

Carnoustie is the most complete examination of every aspect of your game; shot selection and execution, bunker play, ability to recover, course management and putting. A long list that offers every opportunity to turn a one-shot penalty into much worse. It starts at the 1st where any tee shot drifting to the right will leave a totally blind second shot over rough ground and a greenside bunker.

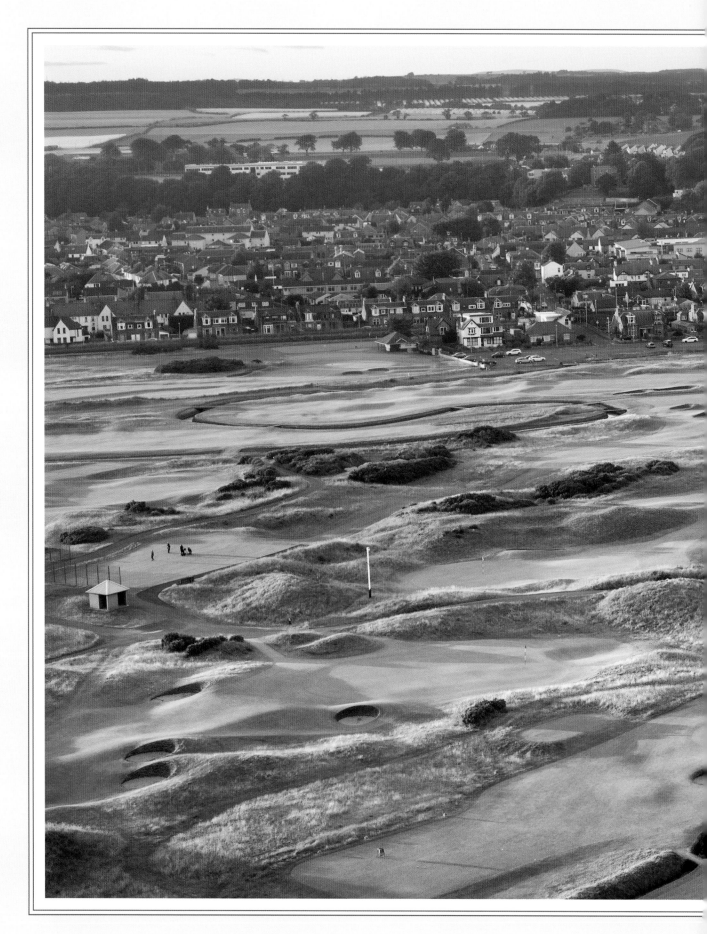

SCOTLAND ¤ *Home of Golf*

The approach to the 3rd green.

CARNOUSTIE | **6** *th*

The 6th is a par five measuring 500 yards, or
more, stroke index 2. There are two possible
lines off the tee; the brave line is between
the left-hand bunker and the out-of-bounds
fence—a narrow channel just 25 yards wide
(Hogan's Alley). The more cautious player
may wish to play further right, to the generous landing area short of the bunkers on the
right. Only the aggressive tee shot will allow
a clear attack to the green and even this is
not without challenge. The green is raised,
long and well protected by bunkers.

Any score of five on this hole should be
judged with satisfaction.

The 5th green and 6th tee to green: Hogan's Alley.

The finish is in sight, the constant examination almost completed. The final three holes are judged one of the toughest finishes in golf, all kicked off by the par three 16th. 245 yards from the back tees, 212 from the forward, frequently into wind, if the distance does not limit you then the table-top green and surrounding bunkers may well.

A three here is an achievement.

Tom Watson won here in 1975 after an 18-hole play-off, he failed to make par on all five visits to the 16th!

CARNOUSTIE | **17**_th_

Carnoustie 17th par four. The penultimate hole is all about the tee shot staying dry but having sufficient length to reduce the approach shot to under 200 yards. The drive should target the island between the two branches of the Barry Burn, 150 yard carry to the first bridge and 240 yard run-out to the second. Depending on how brave you feel getting close to the furthest water, your second shot can be anything up to 230.

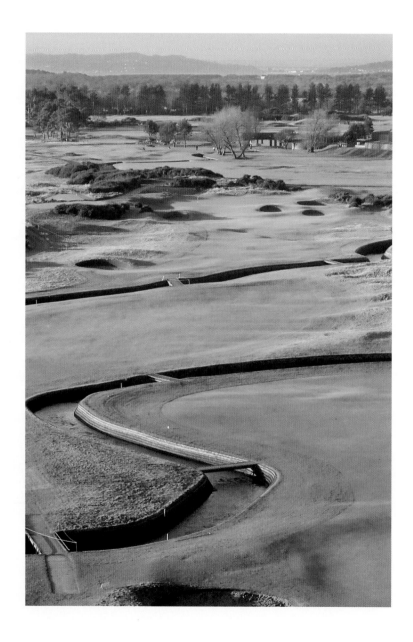

CARNOUSTIE | **18**th

Following on with the theme of this golf course: the 18th is arguably the toughest of finishes.

The drive must consider out-of-bounds to the left, the burn pressing on the right edge of the fairway at 200 yards and fairways bunkers. A good drive should be of 220–250 yards, leaving an intimidating approach that has to carry to the burn.

The Barry Burn runs along the front of the green and is wide, far too wide to hope for a kind bounce just short of it and a hop over—as can happen on the 1st at St Andrews. No matter what has happened during the previous 17 holes, if you are now safely on the putting surface in two, you have a chance for reward and some personal satisfaction.

Many have given description to the challenge of Carnoustie, but I quote the following concise description from nearly 25 years ago:

"It is just depressingly efficient at exposing the weaknesses of one's game" — Tom Doak, *Confidential Guide to Golf*

Kingsbarns

The rise of Kingsbarns Golf Links in its modern iteration can only be described as meteoric. What was farmland just a few short decades ago, is now recognised as one of the finest modern links courses in the world. This is reflected in Kingsbarns' increasingly impressive resume as a tournament venue, from a qualifying course for the St Andrews Open, to co-hosting to the European Tour Dunhill Links Championship for 19 years and hosting its first Major in 2017, the Ricoh Women's British Open.

The record of professional endorsements is matched by the popularity it has achieved with visiting golfers, and it is quoted as the golfers' choice.

Kyle Phillips designed a course that made full use of its coastal location bringing the beach and sea into play on the 3rd, 12th, 15th and 16th holes. Your senses are constantly assaulted by the sound and sight of the North Sea.

However, if its golfing life on the linksland may seem brief, Kingbarns' history runs deep. On the same site the Kingsbarns Golfing Society first played on a nine-hole course as early as 1815. As we can see from the subsequent pictures of societal memorabilia and the following report from a meeting of the society held on 3rd May 1823, membership was a rich and fulfilling experience!

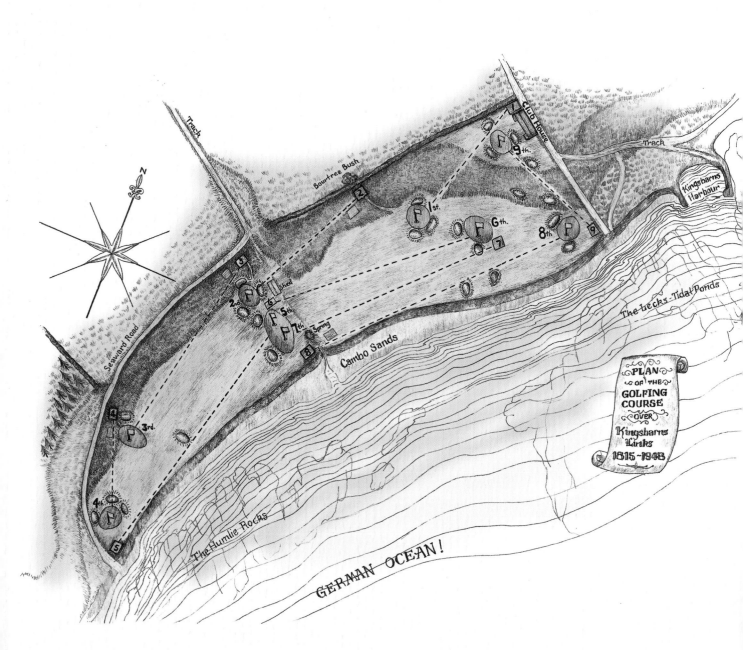

The Humlie Rocks

Cambo Sands

GERMAN OCEAN!

Seaward Road

Track

Bourtree Bush

Club House

Track

Kingsbarns Harbour

The Becks · Tidal Ponds

Spring

Shed

N

PLAN
OF THE
GOLFING
COURSE
OVER
Kingsbarns
Links
1815-1948

The very early 19th century
club medals and snuffbox.

Report from the meeting of the Society held on 3rd May 1823

"The day being favourable, the muster of members was pretty numerous, and several well contested matches were decided. The club sat down to an excellent dinner in the house of Mrs. Brown. The health of the king and many loyal and sentimental toasts were drunk; interspersed by several good songs.

The society proceeded to transact their business by collecting forfeited bets, entering new members and taking on new matches for the meeting; which being concluded, it was unanimously resolved to provide the Society with a medal. After spending the evening with that sociality and harmony which uniformly characterises the Society, the company separated, highly satisfied with the days entertainment."

KINGSBARNS **2**nd

An angry North Sea is the backdrop to the
2nd, a par three playing slightly downhill.

This aerial view shows the par four 7th
followed by the par three 8th, with the
15th on the left and 11th to the right.

KINGSBARNS | **12**_th_

The walk from the back of the 11th green to the 12th tee is a pleasant stroll through trees, over a bridge and then the open view of the sea and 15th tee. A moment of curiosity, a taster of what is to come but time to move on, up the small bank to the par five tee. This elevated position provides a dramatic, panoramic view out to sea, with the flag a distant target and below a generous fairway with no bunkers to threaten an aggressive drive. The challenge here is the second or third shot to a green 70 yards long. Do you throw caution to the wind and risk water, the beach or green-side bunkers or take a more measured approach fifty yards right of the coast and then attack? So much to play for but also—so much to be enjoyed.

The par three 15th tee to green.

An aerial view of Kingsbarns
Golf Links as the sun rises.

This aerial view shows the 16th and 2nd double-green. There are only four single greens—the 1st, 9th, 17th and 18th.

The Old Course

Nine hundred years ago, King David II bequeathed the linksland to the townsfolk of St Andrews—"to do what you see fit". It was a rough peninsula running parallel to the sea and surrounded by Eden Estuary. It was originally called "Muckross", a Pictish name for "Headland of Swine"—or "Land of the Wild Boar" dating at least three-thousand years ago. It sounds like folklore to say the Old Course emerged from this wild patch of thick whinned (gorse) area and rough sandy dunes—but that's what came about.

"Bunkers" were formed by sheltering sheep and cattle through winter storms. Pathways that were trodden by fisherfolk making their way out to the estuary to gather mussels for hand-baiting lines on a daily basis, became "fairways" along with a few flattened areas where rabbits were bred. The Buck Rabbit liked to select the best bit of grass for grazing and scraped a big hole to mark his territory—(that's maybe pushing it a bit far).

It was probably thanks to shepherds, bored by tending their sheep, challenging each other in the 13th Century to see who could reach a dune in fewer swipes using their crook as a club and a stone as a ball. It's man's instinct to compete with one another—it is human nature! In golf just about any country has some sort of similar club and ball game, but because a hole is cut into the ground and a basic set of rules laid down, the Scots claimed the "Gowf".

The first mention that the game was becoming established was when King James II, early in that century, banned golf on the Sabbath, as it interfered with archery practice, which was compulsory for the defence of the realm. One of the first official references to golf on the links was in 1552, in a charter granting Archbishop John Hamilton the right to breed cuniggus (rabbits) there, as long as it did not interfere with locals' rights to play foote-ball or gowf. It was issued by the St Andrews Town Council.

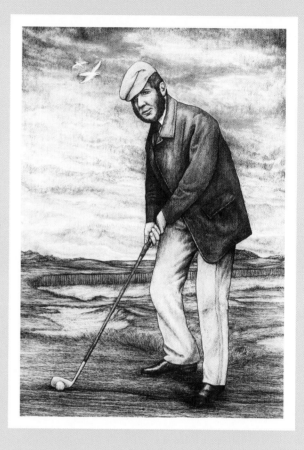

Allan Robertson and Tom Morris, working as ball-makers in St Andrews, were making quite a name for themselves representing their town in foursomes against the Park brothers of Musselburgh and the Dunn brothers of North Berwick. Huge crowds gathered to watch them play. Robertson and Morris were never beaten—in fact Robertson never even lost a game in the annals of time, and was hailed as the undisputed Champion Golfer of Scotland until his untimely death in 1859.

Tom Morris had fallen out with Robertson over the "new-fangled ball" but it was inevitable that it would take over the trade. The new ball was made out of a Malaysian rubber sap and it was much cheaper and easier to make. Robertson and Morris could make two feather balls each on a good day. They were half a crown each—that was half of a man's weekly wage.

Following their disagreement, Morris moved to Prestwick in 1851 to lay out a twelve-hole course which he ran for thirteen years before he was invited back to St Andrews to be Keeper of the Green, Custodian of the Links, in 1864, a position that he held for nearly forty years.

The St Andrews Society of Golfers was formed in 1754, and became the Royal and Ancient Golf Club after royal patronage was given to them by King William in 1834. The Society had adopted thirteen rules for playing the course, which was eleven holes out and the same eleven played back. After just ten years, in 1764, they decided that the first four holes were too short, and adapted them to two holes, and so those recognised nine holes were played up until 1870—playing the nine holes back and giving way on the green to the incoming golfers who had the right of way.

Tom Morris, a born and bred St Andrean, came back to St Andrews in 1864 having been Keeper of the Green at Prestwick for thirteen years. He was given his emblems of office—a barrow, a bucket, a spade, and a salary of £50 per annum, of which he had to pay hired help for carting, scything grass, and filling in rabbit holes. His major job on the Old Course was converting it into eighteen separate holes when the town acquired new ground on what was to become the 2nd to the 7th, and more ground around the loop (still shaped like a shepherd's crook). Morris took advantage and made a feature of the double greens which still impress today. When "the boom" started in the 1850s—people were just jumping off trains and heading straight onto the links. The double greens were there to ease congestion on the way going out and coming in! Morris worked hard and it was ready to play "the modern way" (anti-clockwise) for St Andrews to host its first Open in 1873. It was played in the traditional way (clockwise) on rotation to alleviate wear-and-tear on the course up until the turn of the century when maintenance was minimal. If you're confused, you always play in "the modern way" (anti-clockwise) today. He was responsible for all the major changes that took place on the Old Course for nearly forty years. Morris had a constant fight with tradition against technology—technology against tradition, but stood his ground as golf progressed, and became even more popular by the time he retired in 1902.

Looking back through the 2nd green to the tee and town. The pin, on this upper level, diminishes the threat from the new greenside bunkers, but the wildly undulating approach ground may give an unwelcome bounce to left or right.

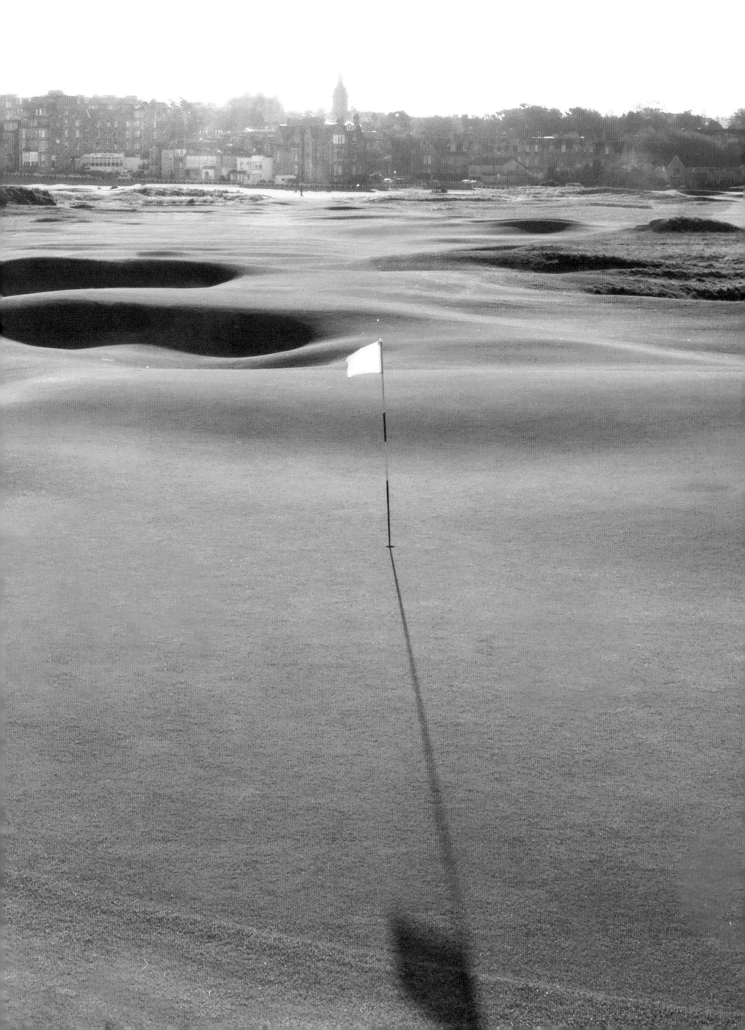

The 4th "Ginger Beer" is a harder driving hole than the previous three. In fact, the second shot, over the mound, and subsequent putting on the undulating green are all equally testing. It was named Ginger Beer after the wheeled basket sent out to this point to provide refreshment in days gone by.

"THE TRIUMVIRATE": Taylor, Vardon, and Braid.

Three very contrasting styles of play, swings, and personalities.

J. H. Taylor and James Braid were both five-time winners of the Open Championship and both double-winners at St Andrews. Harry Vardon was the great innovator of the modern swing (upright and flowing) and the Vardon Grip (overlapping). He won his first Open at Muirfield in 1896, beating Taylor who was favourite to win three in a row. The Committee ruled that they had to play a 36-hole play-off to decide who was the ultimate winner. Vardon went on to become the record holder for the most Open wins. These six championship victories still stand today—one at Muirfield, two at Sandwich, and three at Prestwick.

From 1894 to 1914 "The Triumvirate" accumulated sixteen wins among them and were always in contention until the outbreak of the Great War disturbed the tournament.

ST ANDREWS DOUBLE-WINNERS

J. H. Taylor

Bob Martin, a Scottish golfer from St Andrews. Winner of the Open at St Andrews in 1876 & 1885.

J. H. Taylor is another five-time winner of the Open, also a double winner at St Andrews—1895 & 1900. Co-founder and first Chairman of the British Professional Golfers' Association, the first such association in the world. He continued to compete in the Open long after his final Major win in 1913 at Royal Liverpool achieving 11th in the 1926 Open at Royal Lytham, when he was 55 years old.

James Braid, a five-time winner of the Open, was a double-winner at St Andrews. The first in 1905 and the second, his last major win, in 1910, the 50th Open Championship. He continued to influence and change the game as a prominent golf course architect—Carnoustie and Royal Troon to mention just two included in this book.

James Braid

Jack Nicklaus—18 Major Championship victories, 3 Champion Golfer titles at the Open including back-to-back wins at St Andrews (1970 and 1978). To try to put this in some context; only Tiger has come close to this total, with 15, after that Walter Hagen with 11 and then 9 each for Ben Hogan and Gary Player. Will his total ever be matched?

From his first Major at the Masters Tournament in 1997 to his last also at Augusta in 2019—making **Tiger Woods** both the youngest and second oldest to win the Masters. In between he became a double-winner at the St Andrews Opens, 2000 and 2005.

The history of his shot length, shaping, recovery and putting are well documented but you have to wonder if there will be further Major titles. With Tiger you can never predict, the final chapter may still be written.

Tiger Woods

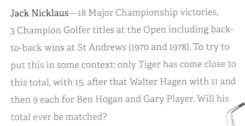

Jack Nicklaus

The 11th, the second and the last par three, is full of history and holds the same dangers now as it did for Jones in 1921. Any tee shot safely on the putting surface is challenged by the severity of the back to front and left to right incline. To the extreme left is Hill bunker, it is here that Bobby Jones' 1921 Open Championship ended.

JONES WINS AT ST ANDREWS IN 1927

In 1927 Mr Robert Tyre Jones, or "Bobby", returned to St Andrews in a blaze of glory, having won the Open Championship the year before at Lytham. He couldn't have had a worse start than on his first visit to Scotland six years previously, when hailed as "The Boy Wonder from the U.S.A.".

His appearance caused quite a stir in the St Andrews Open of 1921—but it turned out to be an anti-climax. A local paper only mentioned, that he retired in the third round, leading all the amateurs after two rounds. On the next day he struggled in a typically hostile Old Course crosswind, going out in 46. He then double-bogeyed the 10th. At the short 11th, he failed to complete the hole.

It was a different story when Bobby Jones returned to challenge the Old Course six years after his disastrous third round in 1921. He opened up with a record-breaking 68 in the first round. Apart from driving into Cheape's bunker off the 2nd tee in three rounds out of four, he was in complete control of the situation. Further rounds of 72, 73, and 72 (it had a par of 73 at that time) saw him win by six shots to become the Open Champion again.

At his Freedom of the Burgh ceremony in 1958, Jones said, "I bunkered my tee-shot into Hill bunker at the 11th. Here I want to correct a bit of history that I read in a St Andrews guide book. I had not played two shots in the bunker then knocked my ball over the green into the River Eden. My ball had come out of the bunker, only in my pocket, and it was my scorecard that made its way into the river."

◆◆◆◆◆◆◆◆◆◆◆◆◆◆◆◆◆◆

THE "GRAND SLAM" 1930

This illustration shows Bobby Jones with the British Amateur Championship at St Andrews. It was the most arduous start in achieving his four "majors" in the one year, for he had to play eight consecutive rounds of match play, winning two of them by just one hole. He admitted to being mentally exhausted by the end of the week.

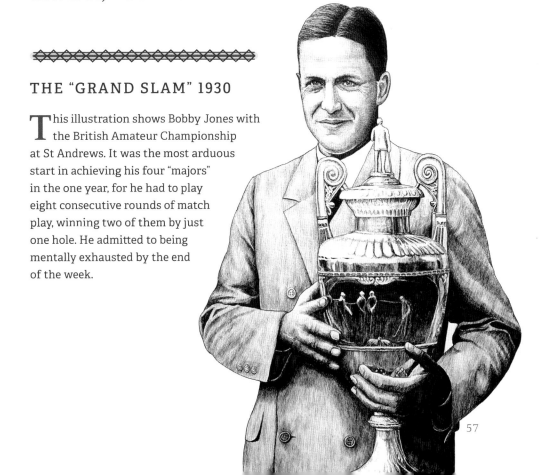

THE OLD COURSE | **14**th

Hell bunker. The 14th, par five, runs slightly above but beside the 5th, also par five. A feature of the Old Course is that the double greens all add up to 18 (2 and 16, etc.) and the double fairways to 19.

The drive is blind to the Beardies, four deep bunkers to the left of fairway, and out-of-bounds to the right. The landing is known as the Elysian Fields and allows a distant view of the flag; what cannot be seen is Hell bunker, 22 paces left-to-right and front-to-back as well as 8 feet tall at the front. Jack Nicklaus' second shot came to rest here in 1995, it took him four shots to escape, the disappointment added to by a three putt finish. Despite walking away with a 10, he made the cut at age 55.

THE OLD COURSE | **16**th

The par four 16th has a number of distractions
and hazards to overcome. Out-of-bounds right,
the Principal's Nose bunkers exactly where
most would like to land their tee shot. The
approach must avoid greenside sand and
mount the raised front to the green, without
falling off the back. It may be difficult to give
this hole the attention it demands—there is,
after all, the 17th next.

THE OLD COURSE | **17**th

The 17th is the most difficult par four on the course, played as a par five until the 1964 Open. It is a famous, iconic golfing challenge, any par score is to be savoured.

A blind tee shot over sheds attached to the hotel, out-of-bounds down the right within the hotel property. Then an approach that must avoid the Road bunker, climb on to a long, narrow green at right angles to the fairway. Remaining on the putting surface and avoiding the road, or worse still, the wall beyond, is a must.

The following aerial image shows the Road hole bottom right.

SCOTLAND □ *Home of Golf*

The late evening light on the longest day shows the undulating 18th fairway and green, and bathes the R&A and town in a golden glow.

THE OLD COURSE | **18**th

The 18th, named 'Tom Morris', provides considerable relief after the testing 17th. An easy drive and approach should offer a birdie chance, the unwary may slide back into the Valley of Sin, to the front of the green. This is a large single green deceptively elevated from the front to back and right to left, putting can be challenging, even from close range and walking away with par or worse can provide the most frustrating of finishes.

St Andrews had become known as "The Home of Golf", with the R&A governing the rules of the game in the 1890s, and Tom Morris becoming known as "The Grand Old Man of Golf".

DUMBARNIE | 6th

The 6th is a par three facing straight out to
the Firth of Forth. The five different tees
all require a full-carry drive, this can vary
between 95 yards for the forward tee and
205 yards from the Championship tee.

Dumbarnie Links

Another major links course has been added in 2020, and heralded as a great asset to the east coast of Scotland and to the "Kingdom of Fife". The Kingdom refers to the kings' domain in the fourteenth century, and the jewel in its crown is now a royal family of links courses to back its name. Now there are over 50 of them of various shapes and sizes in this small county. There are twelve, from a 14 mile trip along the coastline from St Andrews to Dumbarnie.

Dumbarnie Links sits on part of the Balcarres Estate, home of Lord Balneil, whose family have lived here for generations—or should I say centuries. Balneil confirmed his rights by a charter drawn up to include "the right to gowf" around 1580 along with his neighbours, the gentry (gentlemen of recreation and leisure), who claimed for themselves a stretch of prime links from Leven to Lundin Links and Elie.

Back to present day and Clive Clark—the founder and course architect of the project, wanted to design and build a traditional course on a genuine strip of linksland that he could shape and create the impression that it had been there for several decades. Clark has a good pedigree in the game both as a player and architect. He won five European Tour events, was 3rd in the Open in 1967, played in the Walker Cup and the Ryder Cup and was involved in 36 courses in Europe and in America. Clark said, "I have always believed that golf should be fun and a thinking man's game. A good number of holes exhibit "risk and reward"—will you take the heroic line, or will it be safety first?" There are three driveable holes that you might take on and four others where you have that choice of clubs and line. The elevated tees frame an ever changing mood of the sea.

DUMBARNIE | 3rd

This par four tee to green view allows the golfer a clear understanding of the choices, play safe to the generous part of the fairway or pinch as much as possible off the corner.

The safer option allows a clear line to attack the flag. Any aggressive drive falling short of the large bunker leaves a totally blind second shot—risk and reward.

SCOTLAND ▫ *Home of Golf*

DUMBARNIE | **5**th

The par four 5th offers two lines of tee shot, the easier
(right) has less carry, a more generous landing area and a
longer yet less challenging approach to the green; the left
side needs a longer carry and but provides a much shorter
approach. Dumbarnie offers golfers many options off the
tee, all tempting with an element of risk.

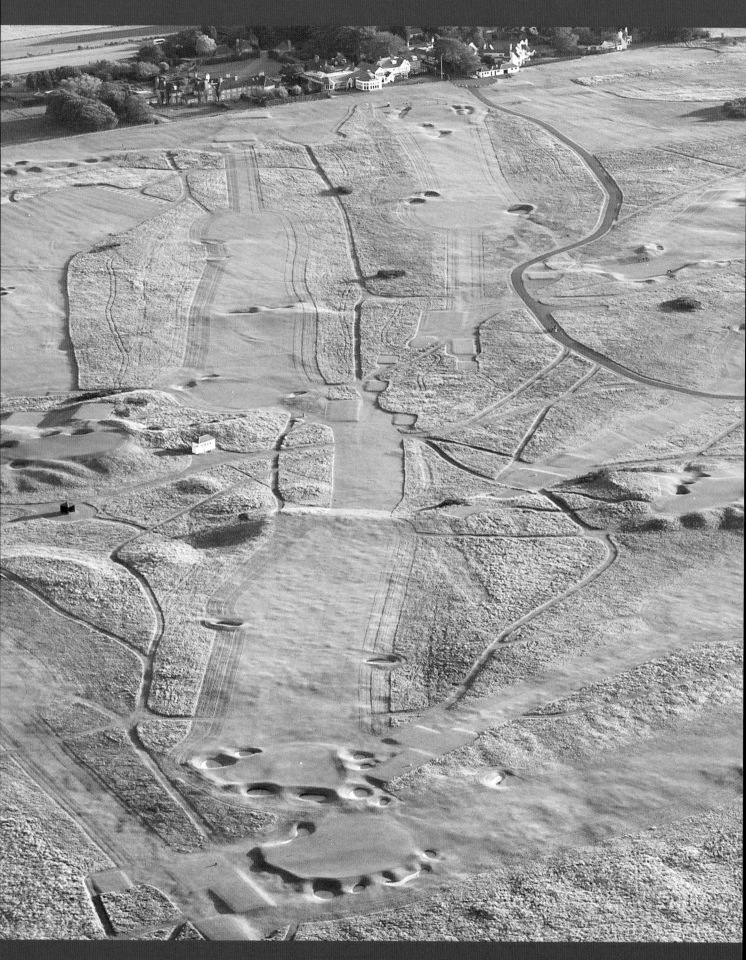

Muirfield

The founders of the Honourable Company of Edinburgh Golfers would have been spotted by shore at Leith Links (near Edinburgh) when it was formed in 1774. Their forefathers confirmed that they had played there, when a rough map of five golfing holes was unearthed dated 200 years before. This was backed up with various references and some really quirky matches or unusual "challenges" by prominent merchants of the capital city early in the sixteenth century.

The company played at Musselburgh from 1824, but through time the course became congested with more clubs formed in and around the nine hole course. The Honourable Company adopted the Edinburgh Club of The Royal Burgess who had drawn up thirteen rules of golf. The rules were pretty basic—for example; "on holing out you will drive a club-length away", later to be changed to two clubs lengths from the hole, which gives you an indication of the conditions of the greens! Another rule—number 11: "if you draw your club; in order to strike and proceed so far unto the stroke as to be bringing down your club; if then your club should break in any way, it is accounted as a stroke".

The Honourable Company who had hosted the six Opens from 1874 had got restless and irritated over the conditions of the course caused by too much play on it. It was still only nine holes and falling behind the game as the numbers playing and the courses grew.

There was a proposal by the members that the Company should move. The area was near the Gullane course where ground was available so Tom Morris was invited to lay down an eighteen-hole course. This proved a problem with the saturation of some of the proposed fairways—it was criticised during construction as being "nothing but a damned water meaddie (meadow)".

The bunker ringed 5th and 11th greens (bottom), the 13th and 17th (right), and 7th and 9th (left) with the 18th and clubhouse centre.

MUIRFIELD | **11**th

The 11th, par four, requires a blind drive over a
ridge. The approach should now be uncomplicated,
through a narrow entrance, but for the heavy
bunkering around all other sides of the green.

The drainage was sorted out to such an extent that the course was ready in 1891, and was to become a surprising host of the Open during dramatic but positive changes for the Championship which were proposed. The first change was to sideline Musselburgh and to introduce Muirfield as the new tournament venue. The second was to increase the play to four rounds over two days. This really did signal the end of Musselburgh. Who would want to play eight times round their nine holes? An entry fee of ten shillings was introduced to help boost the prize money and hopefully to deter the "no hopers" from entering. Up to this point if you were thick-skinned enough, anyone could enter. The Championship despite criticism of the venue was a success. The Scotsman newspaper wrote in 1892, "Muirfield proves good golf, sporting shots, tricky but fair greens".

The first Muirfield winner was an amateur Harold Hilton, who with a swash-buckling style of play, was popular (despite being English!). Prestwick that year had written to the Royal and Ancient in the aftermath of the controversy that this Championship be placed on a much wider basis. They decided to invite two English clubs. The first, St. Georges at Sandwich, hosted the following year, and Royal Liverpool agreed to come on line in the future.

By the time the Open came round again to Muirfield in 1896, the course was lengthened by 800 yards—making it 6,000 yards. "The Triumvirate"—Taylor, Vardon, and Braid, were prominent during the period of 1894 to 1914, and Harry Vardon was victorious in 1896, after a play-off with J.H. Taylor. "The Triumvirate" was again victorious with James Braid winning back-to-back Championships at Muirfield in 1901 and 1906 (Vardon and Taylor were second and third in 1901). A big and powerful pipe-smoking Englishman, Ted Ray, stopped the rot by winning at Muirfield in 1912 with his long-hitting drives (Vardon and Braid were second and third.). Ray went on to win the American Open in 1920.

Muirfield 13th par three

Nicklaus, talking after his win about Muirfield said, "I liked it from the first day I played it. It is essentially a fair course, and has more definition than any links that is played on".

With back-to-back victories in 1987 & 1992, Nick Faldo became only the second man to win two Opens at Muirfield, matching James Braid's achievement nearly a century earlier.

After The Great War disrupted the Championship, Deal, Troon, and Lytham were added to the circuit. Muirfield did not host again until 1929 when Walter Hagen won his fourth title that decade. The Americans were out in force! Apart from the winner, they finished eight out of the top ten. Hagan broke the course record with 67 in the third round.

In 1922, the club had purchased more ground, and hired Harry Colt to redesign Muirfield. Two years later, Tom Morris, long since departed from this earth, would hardly have recognised anything of the original course apart from the old stone dyke (wall) here and there.

When Walter Hagen won in 1929, 274 bunkers had to be avoided during the round, when Ernie Els won there in 2002, there were 148 left.

The start of the emergence with television coverage, reaching the viewers worldwide, and with Gary Player in 1958, and Jack Nicklaus in 1966, Muirfield became internationally known. Muirfield's reputation was further enhanced in the States with wins by Trevino in 1972 and Watson in 1980.

With victory at Muirfield in 2013, Phil Mickelson became just the 12th man in history to win three of the four majors. However, Mickelson's quest for the "career slam" appears destined to be thwarted by the US Open, where he has been runner-up a record six times.

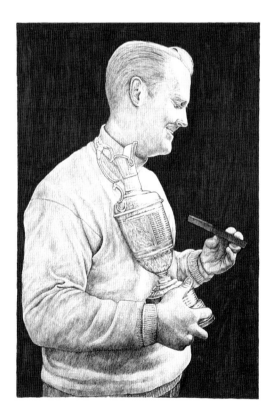

Nicklaus cradles the Claret Jug and admires the medal knowing his 1966 victory at Muirfield sealed his career Grand Slam.

The 1st and 17th in the foreground and on to the 18th. Similar to St Andrews finishing hole, out-of-bounds right but a generous bunker-free fairway to the left.

North Berwick

When the Earls of Fife sponsored a ferry near Elie to take pilgrims back and forth from North Berwick to witness the great construction of St Andrews Cathedral in the twelfth century, a bond was struck between the two Royal burghs. The same pilgrims' badges dating back to 1300 were on sale as souvenirs in both North Berwick and St Andrews for over two centuries! Up to 10,000 people a year were transported across the Forth to visit the saints' relics that were reputedly enshrined in the cathedral. The term "pilgrim" was used loosely; "holidaymaker" would have sounded cheap! With precious little leisure time allotted to the average workingman and his family, a "pilgrimage" was a fine justification for taking a break from the drudgery and monotony of daily life.

The North Berwick Golf Club was founded in 1832, followed by the Tantallon Golf Club in 1853, and with the help of the Bass Rock Club, contributed to the upkeep of the courses. Part of the East Course is the oldest, the West Course is the most celebrated and has been used in qualifying for the Muirfield Open.

Great challenge matches were played over St Andrews, Musselburgh, and North Berwick in the 1850s and '60s. Instead of the arduous, slow journey of the past, attempting to get from one venue to the next, trains had linked up this mini golfing circuit for one and all.

Two-call foursomes being the main form of match play saw the Park brothers of Musselburgh square up to the Dunn twins of North Berwick, or Allan Robertson and Tom Morris representing St Andrews. Over 36 holes on a Saturday, huge crowds turned up for those advertised, much-awaited games and had to be policed because rivalries between the teams' supporters became heated and hostile as the day wore on!

Normally a "challenge" match would be over 12 rounds in six days (24 rounds of the nine-hole North Berwick and Musselburgh courses). Tom Morris and Willie Park played 36 rounds in a confrontation—split equally among the three venues over a three-week period, with just the two Sundays off to get from one course to the next!

The 14th Perfection.

NORTH BERWICK | 15th

The 15th Redan: This is named after a type of fortification, a defence against attack, in that respect this par three is most definitely stoutly defended. The two bunkers facing are clearly visible, just beyond is a deep gully climbing back up to a generously sized green sloping from right to left. Three bunkers lie to the right and one to the left. The bunker on the left can be particularly penal.

One of the most publicised matches at North Berwick was between Tom Morris Snr. and Jnr. against the Park brothers on 6th September in 1875—for a big money purse. Jnr. was reluctant, since he had just married a year ago, and his wife Margaret was heavy with his child—but she persuaded him to go. Young Tom was in his prime, having already won four Opens, at age 24, but Old Tom was not! Although in 1867 he was the oldest winner of the Open—and still is to this day—aged 46. Eight years later for the lead-up to this game he had been struggling with his short game (which he'd always done) with his big goose-necked wooden putter—but this was verging on the dreaded "yips". Anyway, to his relief, Snr. played steadily allowing Jnr. to go for his shots. They were winning easily but hit a bit of sand and the Parks came back at them. They just managed to win on the last green. A telegram arrived saying that Tommy's wife Margaret was struggling in childbirth with his first son, and he had to make his way "post haste" back to St Andrews.

A Mr. Lewis, who had sponsored the match, put his schooner and full crew at the Morris' disposal to take them straight across the Firth of Forth and into St Andrews Bay to be picked up in a rowing boat. As they set sail, unbeknown to them another telegram arrived saying that both his wife and child had died. Sixteen weeks later Young Tom himself passed away on Christmas morning. Reflecting on his life in 1906, Old Tom said mournfully, "people say Young Tommy died of a broken heart, but if that was so . . . I would na' be here either!"

It wasn't just the sadness of Tommy's death—it was what he missed. Courses were springing up all over the country. Parkland courses were now made possible with the manufacture of hand mowers and horses pulling big grass cutters. On reflection, how many Opens would the young man have won? Bearing in mind the opposition against him from 1875, over the following 20 years, he could have been well into double figures in Open Championship wins. Although his life was so dramatically cut short, he has become an almost mythical character in the world of golf.

A year after his death, a subscription was gathered from the fourteen main clubs in existence, and a fine monument erected of Young Tom posing over a putt under the shadow of the square tower in the St Andrews Cathedral grounds.

By this point in your round you will have experienced many totally unique golf holes, in that respect the 16th will not disappoint. At some 370 yards and no fairway bunkers, you may imagine that par will be straightforward. Getting onto the putting surface should, generally, be a task not beyond the ability of most players. However, remaining there or even being on the same half that features the flag could be a matter more of luck than skill. It is narrow, raised and divided in half!

There have been many glowing reports dedicated to this wonderful links course, its uniqueness, quirkiness and most of all fun. Now climbing up the world rankings it still flies under the radar for many.

NORTH BERWICK | **18**th

The final hole bears many similarities with
the 18th at St Andrews. Out-of-bounds right,
a generous landing area left, no bunkers,
a raised front to the green and clubhouse
beyond. It is also a birdie opportunity.

As halfway houses go this lighthouse must provide the most unusual setting. Perched on the clifftop with unrivalled views it offers the perfect place to rest, consider the pleasures of the front nine and contemplate what is to come.

Turnberry

Turnberry has had rather a chequered history, having been first laid out as a private course of thirteen holes for the Marquis of Ailsa on a piece of his land. Willie Fernie, who had just won the Open in 1883, supervised the construction while he was the professional at a small club in Troon, just up the road past Prestwick on the west coast overlooking the Firth of Clyde.

In 1904, the Glasgow and South Western Railway Company persuaded the old marquis to lease them a prime piece of his estate. After two years of building the stunning Turnberry Hotel, the Company added another thirteen-hole course, the "Arran"—named after the island you could see at a distance from the public course. They ran a "Golfers Express" from Glasgow and a direct sleeper service from London to encourage the use of their impressive new golf resort.

Problems arose with the advent of the Great War, when the Royal Flying Corps commandeered the course for a much-needed training facility. After repairing the damage, along came the second war, and the links were flattened to make room for three runways for the Royal Air Force. With wartime nationalisation of the railway, the whole Turnberry complex was under threat. Frank Hole, the hotel manager, successfully appealed to the British Government for compensation to rebuild the courses.

Paul Mackenzie Ross, who had just completed the much-talked about Southerness Links on the west coast, worked with the manager in 1951 to create what was to become an outstanding championship course. For example: a hole like the ninth, "Bruce's Castle", where from this frightening tee, exposed to the elements, in the shadow of a lighthouse, you attempt to drive across the Atlantic Ocean to reach the fairway!

Since the successful new birth of Turnberry it has hosted PGA Match plays, the Walker Cup, the British Amateur, and four Opens. Added to that are the wonderful facilities of the grand old hotel that dominates the landscape.

The new par three 9th tee to green.

Turnberry was the most recent addition to the Open in 1977 with instant fame worldwide, thanks to the drama of the head-to-head between Jack Nicklaus and Tom Watson in the last two rounds, aptly named "The Duel in the Sun". With no-one else remotely in contention, the pair battled it out with spectacular scoring at that time. It was like thirty-six holes of match play, which came down to the final hole, when Watson emerged victorious having scored 65 twice in the third and fourth rounds to big Jack's 65 and 66. The build up of the round, and the outcome, was probably the most memorable one in the history of the Open, and left all the spectators who were lucky enough to witness it . . . exhausted!

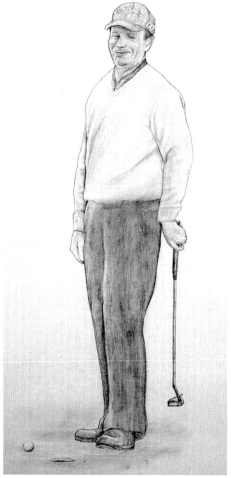

Turn the clock forward to Turnberry thirty-two years later in 2009, where Tom Watson, aged 60, unbelievably had another chance to equal Vardon's six wins and knock "Old Tom" Morris off his perch as the oldest winner by fourteen years! Watson was leading the Open at Turnberry after 71 holes. Oh, it was so nearly the most monumental achievement in the history of the game. Sadly, he was beaten by Stewart Cink in a play-off.

The 17th green to tee.

Turnberry undertook a major re-modelling and opened again in June 2016. All 18 greens were re-laid, several moved much closer to the beach and rocky coastline. Fairways were now defined by the blow-out bunkers while retaining pot bunkers around the greens. The most obvious changes can be seen around the 9th, 10th and 11th. The 9th, now a long par three, maintains the raised tee perched above the ocean. The 10th lengthened to a par five and the 11th tees and green moved to the water's edge. Turnberry, at nearly 7500 yards from the championship tees, has gone from two par fives and four par threes to four par fives and five par threes.

The 15th green, course and distant hotel.

The par three 11th green to tee.

SCOTLAND ¤ *Home of Golf*

Greg Norman won his first Major in 1986 with a score of level par, 12 strokes higher than Tom Watson's Duel in the Sun win. The weather conditions, on the first day, were particularly bad with constant rain and wind. Norman described the day as a brutal experience. He produced a 63 the following day and had an eventual winning margin of 5 shots over Gordon Brand Jnr.

TURNBERRY | **18**_th_

The 18th has seen more than its fair share of
Open Championship drama on the four occasions
it has played host. Although Turnberry is a different course today from that of previous battles, it
is designed to continue to at least maintain that
tradition if it is included in the Open rota.

An aerial image showing the
par four 17th, 18th and clubhouse.

Prestwick   *Birthplace of the Open*

"Please send a respectable caddie to represent their club to compete in a challenge belt of 3 twelve-hole rounds of stroke play over Prestwick on the 12th October to decide who will be the Champion Golfer of the Year", wrote the secretary to Blackheath, Perth, Bruntsfield, Musselburgh, and St Andrews.

And so the Open was born in 1860. That invitation may have sounded patronising, and indeed it was! The early years of the Open were just a form of entertainment for the members of the Club after the Autumn Meeting.

The Earl of Eglinton presented an impressive belt for the Open of soft red Moroccan leather with a detailed golfing scene engraved on its silver buckle. It was the type of trophy he might have competed for jousting or in archery some thirty years earlier. The Earl stipulated that if the belt was won three years in a row it was yours to keep. He had become the first official sponsor

Willie Park Senior, winner of the first Open Championship at Prestwick in 1860.

of a professional golf tournament when the eight competitors lined up in heavy green checked foresters' jackets—normally worn by workers on his estate. The winner of the first Championship was Willie Park from Musselburgh and Tom Morris representing Prestwick was runner-up.

The length of the course at that time was 3,799 yards, the longest hole being the 1st at 578 yards, formidable, as the average drive of a crack professional was between 180 and 200 yards almost (all carry with very little run on the ball). When Tom Morris Jnr. was going for his third Open Championship in a row in 1870—while still a teenager—he eagled the first in the opening round, which was awesome with the equipment he used at that time. He defended the belt winning by twelve shots and so it was his to keep!

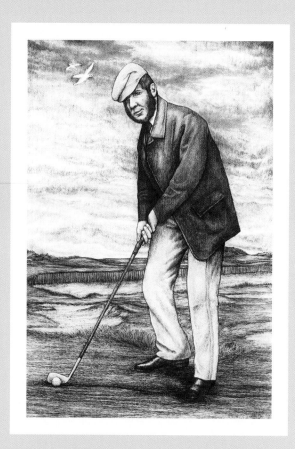

There can surely never be a more successful father and son than the Morris's.

Old Tom is the oldest winner of a Major aged 46, he won the Open 1861, 1862, 1864 and 1867

Young Tom, the youngest winner of a Major aged just 17, he won the Open in 1868, 1869, 1870 and 1872

The shortest hole, the 11th, was recorded at 97 yards. Many of the holes were a blind shot from the tee to the green as sand hills or dunes had to be "lofted" over. As usual, it was imperative to keep the ball in play as there were no preferred lies dictated by one of the 13 basic rules laid down.

It's a familiar story by now on this Scottish coastal trail that the railway, in this case the Glasgow and Southwest, linked up the thriving city of Glasgow to Ayr in 1849. The Earl of Eglinton, who owned substantial grounds and a castle, waved down the first trains from Glasgow that steamed through his estate and demanded free rides down to Ayr and back—as was his right. He had access to a patch of rough linksland about three miles to the north of Ayr and decided now that he had "transport", it would be an idea to invite Tom Morris across to lay out a proper course at Prestwick. The Earl's great friend and foursomes partner, James Ogilvie Fairlie (captain of the Royal and Ancient in St Andrews at that time), persuaded Morris to move to Prestwick with his family to become "keeper of the green"—a position old Tom would hold for 13 years before returning to St Andrews and maintaining the Old Course for 38 years.

Morris was to lay out 12 holes in a cramped and restricted area, but took full advantage of the contours and ambience of the site that included stunning views across the sea to the Isle of Arran. Shortly before he started work, 50 members, newly enrolled by Fairlie, met for the first time in 1851 in the Red Lion Inn, just a drive and a cleek from the proposed course. The early days of the Prestwick club were "troubled", as by scanning the minutes of the secretaries' reports in the 1850s there seemed to be a great reluctance by the membership to pay their annual subscription of a pound!

Tom Morris worked tirelessly to improve the course. He found that sand was a great protector of links turf against biting winds and hard frost. He discovered this by accident by spilling a barrowload of it at the side of a green he was having trouble establishing. Having spread the sand around instead of shovelling it back into his barrow, he found that over the winter the grass around this area seemed to revive itself. From that moment on top-dressing became a standard greenkeeping practice and "sand ... more sand!" was to be the Morris battle cry or instruction on every links course he was involved with from then on.

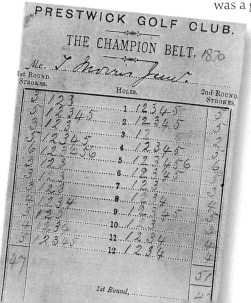

The 1870 scorecard of Young Tom Morris when he scored a three on the 1st hole, measuring 578 yards.

PRESTWICK | 3rd

The par five 3rd is a dogleg right, over Cardinal
bunkers, to a rumpled fairway. Only the longest
tee shots can attack the green in two but beware
the out-of-bounds Pow Burn.

A n aerial view of the 17th green to tee
(lower left) with the 15th green above it.
To the right the 2nd tee to green, par three.

Prestwick 17th Sahara.

The great golf writer Bernard Darwin said at the time, "I gravely doubt whether a championship should be played here again. Golf can be altogether too popular"... and so it was to be—despite being the original home of the Open, the club did not ask to be its host again.

This aerial image (opposite) shows 17 greens, 18 tees and 18 fairways. Just the 7th green is missing. It clearly shows the lack of space for Prestwick to accommodate large crowds and the Open Championship infrastructure.

It may seem short by today's standards but the design, the placement of tees, greens, bunkers and the naturally undulating ground, is so good that it will test even the most proficient golfer. Yes, there are blind shots but a good caddie and the confidence of your stroke will see you through. It is a walk back in time on a course presented to 21st century conditions. Give yourself time to enjoy the warm hospitality of the clubhouse, maybe both before and after your round!

Harry Vardon holds the record for Open Championship wins, six of them, having won at Prestwick three times. He was widely regarded as the best player in the world since Young Tom Morris. He attended The US Open on three occasions, beating J. H. Taylor to win in 1900. His status was such that in 1937 The Vardon Trophy / Harry Vardon Trophy was created to be awarded annually by the US PGA/European Tour to their leading low score player. Starting from 1937 it shows the greatest players on both sides of the Atlantic, These two lists of winners is a pleasant reminder of the greats of days gone by—except in one respect—Jack Nicklaus. With 18 Majors, 74 Tour wins and the leading low-scorer on eight occasions, he failed to play the required number of rounds to qualify.

Royal Troon

Troon is the only "Royal" on the west coast, having been so honoured in 1978 during its 100th Anniversary by Her Majesty Queen Elizabeth II. The Troon Club was founded with just twenty golfers—but twenty years later had grown to seven hundred playing members. There was an amazing surge of players and courses from this moment in 1898 till it calmed down in about 1910. Willie Fernie, Troon's club professional converted their course from 12 to 18 holes in 1888, by then, the recognised standard of holes played (not the number of "nips" in a bottle of whisky). The overall yardage was 5,656 as compared to over 7,000 yards today. It boasts the longest and the legendary shortest hole, the "Postage Stamp", spanning over 90 years in Open Championship golf.

When Troon was secure and becoming well established in the 1890s they were surrounded by "the winds of change"—the changing of playclubs (drivers), to the changing shape of the swing; even the change of the original hammer grip (featured in this Troon section) to the introduction of golf bags which caused great consternation within the ranks of caddies throughout all of Scotland.

The "American Invasion" and the dominance in particular of Walter Hagen and Bobby Jones at the Opens in the 1920s was briefly interrupted in 1923 at Troon. Englishman Arthur Havers held off Hagen, the defending champion, by a single shot. Hagen, who was to win four times up to 1929, was irritated that professionals were not allowed in the Troon clubhouse. Invited in just for the presentation of the claret jug, he declined and chose to invite any of the spectators to the local pub who fancied a pint! Only two Americans came over for the next Open at Troon in 1950, and they were both amateurs. Bobby Locke from South Africa, winning by two shots, successfully defended the

Bobby Locke, a four-time Open Champion including 1950 at Royal Troon.

Defending Champion Arnold Palmer dominated the course and the field during his 1962 win at Royal Troon.

title he had won at Sandwich. With the American Tour established, the Open failed to attract the leading players until Arnold Palmer breathed life back into it when he just failed to win at St Andrews in the Centenary Open.

By the time Palmer strode onto the first tee at Troon in 1962, the crowds were back and television had made it international viewing. Having won at Birkdale the year before, Palmer dominated the Troon championship, leaving all in his wake. His St Andrews caddie of 35 years, "Tip" Anderson, said that it was the best he had ever seen "Mr. Palmer" play. With rounds of 71, 69, 67, and 69 on hard fairways, thick rough, and fast greens, only Kel Nagle got within six shots of him with third-placed Phil Rodgers 13 shots behind.

Tom Weiskopf matched Palmer's aggregate of 276 when the Open returned to Troon in 1973. Locked in battle with Johnny Miller in the third and fourth rounds and with Nicklaus making one of his memorable "charges" in the last round, Weiskopf, who had opening rounds of 68 and 67, held on to win. Tom Watson added a fourth of five Open Championships at the height of his illustrious career in 1982—the same year he won the U.S. Open. Arnold Palmer was made an honorary member of Royal Troon Golf Club that year.

Six Troon Opens in a row had been won by Americans: Palmer, Weiskopf, Watson, Mark Calcavecchia in 1989, Justin Leonard in 1997, and a surprise winner Todd Hamilton, who beat Ernie Els in a play-off in 2004. Todd had made the entry for the Open by finishing 2nd in the Japan Tour. Henrik Stenson, who is Swedish, stopped yet another American win, by beating Phil Mickelson in a head-to-head battle on a memorable Troon last day in 2016.

During the Centenary Open at St Andrews, James Braid, architect for the Royal Troon golf course, met Arthur Havers, the first Open winner in 1923.

ROYAL TROON | 8th

Looking down on to the 8th green
(Postage Stamp) ringed by bunkers.
Even from this close position the
target does seem rather small.

W alter Hagen achieved 11 Majors, including four Open Championship victories. Runner-up to Arthur Havers by one shot in 1923 , Hagen was irritated that professional competitors were not allowed into the Troon clubhouse apart from the presentation ceremony, which he declined to attend.

Royal Troon 18th green and clubhouse.

ROYAL TROON | **18***th*

Royal Troon is a traditional links course: straight out, a bit of a meander around the turn and then straight back. The most attractive six holes are from the 7th, winding through and around small sandhills to provide some welcome land movement and visual variety. It is widely judged a good test of golf, difficult, but not one that is particularly attractive.

Castle Stuart 18th, clubhouse and course.

Castle Stuart

Castle Stuart is a new course, opened in 2009. Although it's housed in the "Scottish Highlands," it is a seaside links, about 6 miles from Inverness on the banks of the Moray Firth on its way up to Dornoch. It has certainly made an impact in a very short time, hosting four Scottish Opens already.

Phil Mickelson won there one week before he went on to win the Open at Muirfield in 2013. He said, "it was exactly what I needed, to win in Castle Stuart, it gave me confidence I could play my best golf in links conditions."

It was co-designed by two Americans, Mark Parsinen and course architect Gill Hanse. Both were involved in big projects in the past in Scotland. Mark was responsible for overseeing the construction and establishing Kingsbarns (featured in this book). Gill designed a new course "Craighead" running parallel to the old Crail Links. For the opening in 1999, I was invited to talk about the old days, (dressed as "Old Tom" Morris) when he laid out and converted Crail in 1892. Hanse and Morris then did a question-and-answer session for the members. Old Tom tried persistently to find out what Hanse had been paid for the new course—but to no avail!

Castle Stuart is a restored tower house. The castle and land the course was built on were granted to James Stewart, 1st Earl of Moray, by his half-sister, Mary Queen of Scots following her return to Scotland from France in 1561. She would have approved of this course, as she was the first woman to be seen playing golf. In fact the Queen caused much concern, when she was reported to be playing on the links of Seaton (near Edinburgh) one week after the death of her husband Lord Darnley—which made many of her loyal subjects . . . "suspicious!".

The course is in two loops linked by an art-deco clubhouse on a rugged landscape of gorse, heather and sea grass. Mark Parsinen said, "Castle Stuart is not a kick through the uprights type of course—it is not like so many traditional links courses that play between sand dunes but rather has an open style with minimal bunkering". Instead, used through the entire layout are expansive, wild-looking waste bunker areas, giving a wonderful feeling "of days gone by" to the course.

CASTLE STUART | 3rd

The 3rd is a drivable par four, on most days. If the two shot option is preferred, the drive should favour the right-side of the fairway. The green is long, narrow and has a gentle incline towards the water.

This aerial view shows the par three 8th, bottom right, with the 7th above. The 2nd and 3rd shoreline holes are also visible as is the 6th green to the left.

The par four 10th and par three 11th greens.

CASTLE STUART | **18**th

The 18th is a par five that seems to tempt an aggressive second shot directly at the green. There is a hidden fairway area beyond the left-side of the large waste bunker. This is the largest green on the course which can be both a benefit and a hindrance.

The par four 4th, 400 yards to this most unusual and challenging shaped green.

Royal Dornoch

The Triumvirate of Vardon, Taylor and Braid were unanimous in their praise for the links of Royal Dornoch. People took notice—so impressed was J.H. Taylor that he chose to spend a two week holiday each year in Dornoch during the height of his career. One hundred years later another five times winner of the Open, Tom Watson, is equally lavish with his praise for the course. Had it not been so far "off the beaten track" it might well have hosted the Open Championship by now.

King Edward VII granted a Royal charter to Dornoch Golf Club in 1906. He often stayed with his friend the Duke of Sutherland in the stately Dunrobin Castle and with Andrew Carnegie, a Scotsman who made his fortune in America as a steel magnate and philanthropist. He had spent a fortune near Dornoch rebuilding Skibo Castle and turned it into one of the world's great residences.

The king and his pals often played a foursome joining John Sutherland on the links. Sutherland became synonymous with Dornoch. He became the club secretary in 1883, a position he would hold for 50 years. His reputation and knowledge of the game was such that he was invited to write for Golf Illustrated at the turn of the century—which helped profile and publicise the town and the links. He had made a big impact, for within two years of becoming secretary, Sutherland had invited Tom Morris up to convert and extend the original nine holes to eighteen in 1886. Morris remarked after he'd completed the layout that there was nowhere better to be found for golf, as many have said since. He was particularly impressed with the numerous small plateaux, or table hillocks, some of which he turned into square greens.

Sir Robert Gordon, tutor to the young Earl of Sutherland in 1616, wrote "along the seacoast at Dornoch were the fairest and largest links of green fields in any part of Scotland". They were equal to St Andrews for golf and

ROYAL DORNOCH | **5**th

During the dry, fast running conditions of summer, this par four may be reachable with a gentle following wind—but getting up on to the putting surface is almost impossible. In fact, long drives may add to the difficulty by being so close to the elevated green that they cannot even see the flag. The aerial view shows that this is a long green with two wicked, deep sand bunkers on the left side. The challenge continues on to the par three 6th beyond.

archery and compared favourably with Montrose, Leith, Musselburgh and Scotscraig as a venue for race meetings—"horses for courses!".

In 1902 the railway connected to Dornoch, and making use of the sleeping car service from London to Inverness was set to become a fashionable and desirable location for the long distance "trainset" and the town welcomed Londoners with status and wealth.

American golfers that know a bit of history about the game in the States, will be familiar with the name Donald Ross who became a prominent course designer, including Number Two at Pinehurst in North Carolina. He was born and bred in Dornoch but left aged eighteen to learn about the art of club making with Forgans of St Andrews. He had followed Tom Morris as a

boy watching him supervising laying out the greens on his home course. "Old Tom" was impressed with his enthusiasm and took Ross under his wing when he arrived in St Andrews on an extensive period of course design of which Morris walked every venue accompanied by young Ross, including touring England (Newcastle and Wallasey), Ireland (Royal County Down, Lahinch and Rosapenna) and Scotland (Muirfield and Dunbar). That was an impressive apprenticeship, but he went back to Dornoch as greenkeeper and put his experiences to good use before being lured away to Boston at the turn of the century. His brother Alex went with him and won the U.S. Open in 1907! Donald Ross became a prolific course designer and at one point in 1925 had over 3,000 men gainfully employed in his constructions.

ROYAL DORNOCH | **10**th

The 10th, at just 140 yards, should be less troublesome than the yardage suggests. All carry, unless you are very good at running the ball through either of the very narrow gaps in the bunkers, and then hope for the centre of the green—left, right or long will require a deft touch and a slice of luck if par is to be achieved.

The par five, 500 yard, 12th green.

Then the par three 13th and Foxy, the 14th.

ROYAL DORNOCH | **14**_{th} *Foxy*

So much has been written about Foxy, it would
seem a universally popular yet demanding
golf-hole; 445 yards, par four; no bunkers and
a wide enough fairway. The approach is to a
green that sits at a right angle to the fairway
and nearly pointed at that edge. Any flag placed
in that first 30 feet of green should not be a
target, in fact, I suspect, the wise advice may be
to go for the middle of the green, regardless of
where the flag is. At least then you will have
a crack at par or better.

ROYAL DORNOCH | 15*th*

The par four 15th crosses
wildly undulating ground,
around hairy mounds and
on to an elevated green.

The table-top, par three
11th green—at 140 yards

Cruden Bay

In recent times, the award-winning American architect Pete Dye described Cruden Bay as "outsized, nonconformist, unpredictable, flamboyant—certainly among the top 10 courses of Scotland that on no account should be missed." One hundred years earlier, Harry Vardon won the first professional tournament held in Cruden Bay which had attracted huge crowds. Vardon was in his prime in 1899 and had successfully defended his title as the Open Champion. Bernard Darwin, the noted golf writer, was following the day's play and reported on the course saying, "Some of the shots are blind if you like to call it so . . . but there are also some truly fine golfing holes on the grand scale".

Tom Morris was asked to lay out a course which would attract visitors from afar. He must have been gleeful as he looked down on the east coast cliff at the proposed ground that appeared. It was the best birds–eye view ever. Morris who prided himself on walking every venue thoroughly and inspected every nook and cranny, would have had a seat on the site of the proposed clubhouse and just looked! On such a quirky piece of linksland he took full advantage of its natural but unpredictable terrain of bumps and humps and threaded his way through all its eccentricities. The ploy for Cruden Bay was to attract holidaymakers to the luxurious Great North Railway Hotel, promoting itself as "A health resort with sandy dunes and an excellent golf course". It did well but after the Depression in the early thirties it could not justify keeping up the once regal Cruden Bay Hotel image.

Before the slump in 1926 Tom Simpson, an English golf architect, was invited up to revamp the course. It was a good choice for he was as eccentric as the course! Simpson was no fool having constructed some major courses in Belgium, France, Spain and Ireland and avoided "change for the sake of change" and he highlighted all its quirky ways.

I am well aware that I keep on mentioning Tom Morris throughout this book—because I have to!

He was involved with every aspect of the game and was responsible for the majority of the old courses we have highlighted in *Scotland—Home of Golf.*

Morris lived through the major transitions (1821 to 1908) in the evolution of the game. Morris Snr. played in 36 consecutive Opens and was the first sports legend in his own time, known latterly as the Grand Old Man of Golf. He laid out over 80 courses, kept a club-making shop for over forty years beside the 18th green and kept up with all the dramatic changes up until his retirement in 1902.

A low level aerial view of the fiercely
bunkered, table-top par three 11th green.

CRUDEN BAY | **6**th

The par five 6th at over 500 yards presents a testing approach shot, regardless of what number you are hitting.

Back-to-back par threes, the 15th and 16th, the latter from an elevated tee to the distant green.

This aerial image shows the 12th green,
huge dunes and distant clubhouse.

Trump International

Dr. Martin Hawtree, the highly respected golf architect, said, "My speech is out here on the course. I think when you go round it and play you will find it is one of the most extraordinary golf links sites you have ever seen, or you will ever see." One of the wisest moves that Mr Trump had made was to promote Hawtree from "links consultant" to "lead designer" of the project. It was to prove invaluable, drawing on all his experience as he threaded his way through the towering dunes. It occupies a three-mile stretch of classic golfing terrain—and shares the privileged company of the highly reputed Royal Aberdeen and Cruden Bay courses.

The par four 14th tee to green.

SCOTLAND ◻ *Home of Golf*

There can surely be a no more naturally formed area of linksland as this. Pictured left to right—the 17th, 12th and 13th flags

The 5th, 6th, 7th, 8th & 9th from the air.

Royal Aberdeen

The ancient links of Aberdeen, along with those of Leith near Edinburgh, had rough charted maps of both of their five-hole courses, which still survive to confirm their early existence. In the 1640s there was enough interest in playing the game to merit John Dickson being granted a permit from the council of the city to exercise the trade of making golf balls for the community.

1620 was the first record anywhere in Scotland of "actual holes" being on a course. In the Aberdeen reference no indication of their size is mentioned, but there again they varied from a small hole scraped out with a knife, ending up a size of a Balmoral bonnet on a busy medal day! This was caused by scooping the earth or sand out of the hole by hand and creating a mound to tee off on. A wily member of the Society of Golfers at Aberdeen (founded in 1780) might well have applied for a late tee time in the hope of holing a few more putts as the size of hole became more "sociable" (got bigger and bigger) on the way round. The club, after 100 years of playing on the town's links, decided to move to new ground just to the North of the river Don's estuary. The town's links had become severely congested with locals exercising their right to play football and cricket, to parade, and even hang their salmon nets to dry on it.

The design work of James Braid, a common feature throughout this book, is again on show here at Royal Aberdeen. The course you play today is largely his work where you will be tested but fairly treated.

George Duncan had a fine flow-ing swing as you can see in my illustration hitting a fairway wood.

In view the 4th, 5th, 6th, 8th and 9th flags and occasional hint of bunkers, from ground level. Tees and fairways remain hidden in the rolling dune structures. Widely regarded as one of the finest front nines in golf.

It proved to be a good move to one of the most spectacular sites in Scottish links golf. The opening hole plays directly toward the sea, the routing then turns directly along the shoreline and, playing inside the protection of high sand dunes, offers a variety of challenging holes that utilise all the dramatic variation of nature's landscaping. Even though the back nine's return is further back from the sea, their elevated position offers you sea views and continuing challenge. This a venue worthy of far more recognition that it receives.

Aberdeen's George Duncan was the best-known home-grown professional. He won the Open in the first Championship after the Great War at Deal in 1920. Duncan was probably the quickest golf player in golf—colourful in his fashionable attire, and in his style of play. His book "Golf at the Gallop", was a huge success. He would have found today's play irksome—to say the least! Duncan would simply walk to his ball, drop his limbs into his stance and immediately hit the ball. If he ever studied the line and shape of the shot, he had done it before he reached his ball, for there was no pause when he got to it. As for practice swings, he regarded them as totally unnecessary and barely legal. He was a formidable match player and he represented Great Britain versus the United States in the early Ryder Cups and never lost in any singles matches over three venues of their matches. He picked up an Irish and two French Opens.

Looking back through the 6th green.

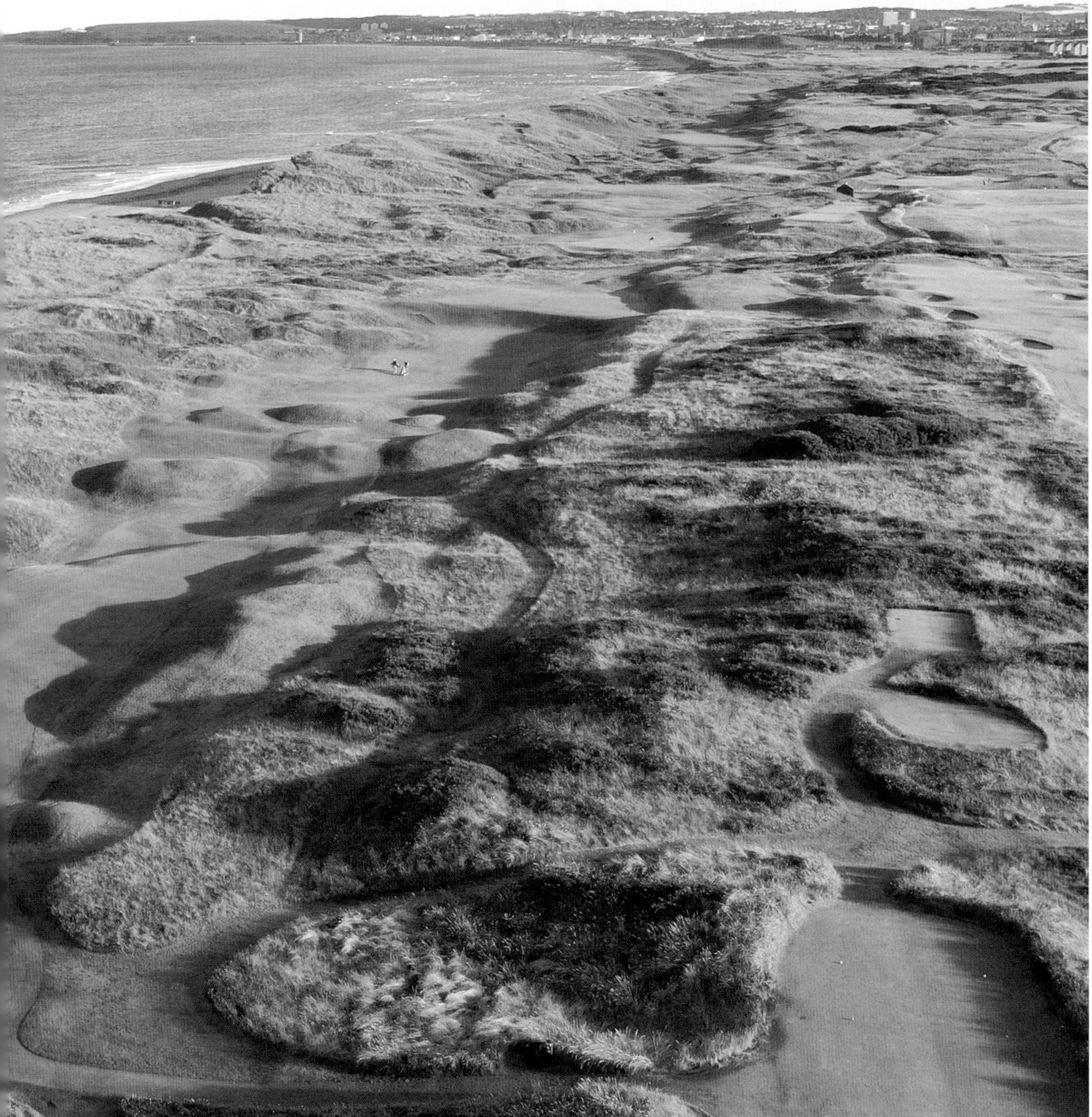

ROYAL ABERDEEN | **8**th

Ten bunkers await any wayward tee shot on
the par three 8th. This signature hole can
play anything from a wedge to a long iron
depending on wind direction and strength.

Royal Aberdeen back nine is on an upper level. Here is the 13th, Blind due to its blind tee shot and sometimes second shot, also the 14th and 15th.

The 18th is judged one of the most difficult holes on the course. At over 400 yards, and frequently in to wind, it requires a long and accurate drive to avoid out-of-bounds left and fairway bunkers pictured. The green is raised and well bunkered, although not many will be taking it on in two.

SCOTLAND □ *Home of Golf*

Epilogue

That concludes this presentation of our selected fourteen golf courses and the players who have entertained us, shaped the game and, through their play, pushed the boundaries of the impossible. I have to confess that in selecting the courses you have so far seen, I felt some guilt at those not featured—well-known names that have given pleasure to many tens of thousands of visiting golfers over the decades.

Of course, to try to add to a "top" list, of anything, risks diluting the original message—and how many do you add, where do you stop; after all we are not short of great links courses?

Disregarding that concern, I offer the following, just a taster of what else we have to offer.

This view of the par three 13th tee to green.

Brora

A course was first laid out here by Old Tom Morris in 1891 but it was James Braid who later transformed it to the course you see today. It opened in 1923.

If peace and tranquillity, away from noise and distraction, is your desire . . . then Brora may not be for you. The on-course residents, cattle and sheep, are noisy eaters and stare a lot, which can be disconcerting! You will also see the greens are ringed by electric fences (step over them carefully!), to keep the non-players off the putting surface.

However, if you seek a wonderful, challenging and largely unchanged course, framed between highlands and water (the North Sea), then this it. The fun of the course is matched by the warm welcome in the clubhouse, and the strength of its membership, locally, nationally and internationally is proof of that. You may well fall in love with this course and be drawn back again, many times.

This view of the 9th approach, par four.

Gleneagles

Gleneagles may feel like it is set in the heart of the Highlands, but in fact it's only a one-hour drive from St Andrews.

From its earliest days the Gleneagles estate has been a destination of the rich and famous, royalty and sophisticates alike. That continues to this day with a 5-star hotel that retains the epic grandeur of the roaring 20's along with an award-winning Spa and the only 2 Michelin star restaurant in the country.

Gleneagles boasts three eighteen-hole Championship golf courses, a luxury five-star hotel and activities to excite and entertain. James Braid laid out the King's (1919) and Queen's (1917), Jack Nicklaus designed the PGA Centenary course, host to the 2014 Ryder Cup. Of the three, the Kings is the stand-out course as it winds through natural land movements to give an ever-changing backdrop and variety of challenge.

Crail

Crail Golfing Society was formed in 1786, the seventh oldest golf club in the world. They acquired the new Balcomie ground in 1894 and invited Old Tom to lay out a new nine-hole course, he returned to lengthen it in 1900. This is another course that is full of fun, playing around the coast and then back on a slightly inland route.

Two par threes have achieved a reputation: the "over a hill" 13th measuring 200 yds to an undulating green, then a 180 degree change of direction to the 140 yard downhill 14th, pictured. The building in the background is the disused old lifeboat house, make of that as you will.

Elie

Elie, or the Golf House Club as it is known, isn't just unique by name. How many other courses have a submarine periscope on the 1st tee? The course lies thirty minutes' drive south of St Andrews and looks out over the Firth of Forth to Edinburgh. This is where five times Open Champion James Braid grew up and learnt his golf. Given how good this golf course is, it does fly under the radar, and will surprise and delight those who visit. A true links test with some lovely seaside holes, undulating fairways and the occasional blind shot, but you should never feel unfairly treated.

This is the final golf course image, in normal playing conditions. It is the approach to the short par four 10th, blind from the tee, the marker

pole providing driving direction.
Any drive of 200+ yards will reach
the top of this incline and give a clear
view of the green, the down slope
being an aid to further distance.
Any drive over 280 yards will be on
the beach or in the sea—just when
is high water?

W inter sets in. The old grey toon—the
hotels, apartments and houses seem
to huddle together for warmth, all except the
R&A that stands watch over the Old Course.

Dawn on the links.